BOOKS BY MARVIN BELL

THE ESCAPE
INTO YOU

THE ESCAPE

New York

ATHENEUM

1971

MARVIN BELL

INTO YOU

A sequence

Acknowledgments are due the following publications in whose pages some of these poems previously appeared: CONCERNING POETRY, FIELD, HEARSE, THE IOWA REVIEW, THE MAJOR YOUNG POETS (World), THE NATION, NEW AMERICAN REVIEW, THE NEW YORKER, THE NORTH AMERICAN REVIEW, NORTHWEST REVIEW, POETRY, and THE VIRGINIA QUARTERLY REVIEW.

The following poems appeared originally in POETRY: *Constant Feelings; The Daily Grind; The Drifting; The Escape into You; Getting Lost in Nazi Germany; Homage to Alfred Stieglitz; In the Home; Lovesong; The Music of the Spheres; Put Back the Dark; The Ring; and Service for Two.*

Song: The Organic Years appeared originally in THE NEW YORKER.

PUBLISHED SIMULTANEOUSLY IN CANADA BY MC CLELLAND AND STEWART LTD.

MANUFACTURED IN THE UNITED STATES OF AMERICA

COMPOSITION BY KINGSPORT PRESS, INC., KINGSPORT, TENNESSEE

PRINTED AND BOUND BY THE MURRAY PRINTING COMPANY

FORGE VILLAGE, MASSACHUSETTS

DESIGNED BY KATHLEEN CAREY

FIRST EDITION

DOROTHY

CONTENTS

I HOMAGE TO THE RUNNER

II THE ESCAPE INTO YOU

III THE DAILY GRIND

IV *ON UTILITARIANISM*

V *INTERLUDE: INSTRUMENTS OF THE LORD*

VI *CONSTANT FEELINGS*

Love is too young to know what conscience is;
Yet who knows not conscience is born of love?
SONNET CLI

If I can think of it, it isn't what I want.
Randall Jarrell, A SICK CHILD

I

HOMAGE TO THE RUNNER

HOMAGE TO THE RUNNER

The form of this "sport" is pain,
riding up into it, he hurts to win.
These are the moments when death is really
possible, when a man can fit into
his enlarged heart all that is known
or was or shall be pumping fulfills.

The love of form is a black occasion
through which some light must show
in a hundred years of commitment.
By the time the body aches to end it,
the poem begins, at first in darkness,
surrounded by counterfeits of leisure.

Run away. Leave them to ease.
What does it matter you wind up alone?
There is no finish; you can stop for no one.
When your wife cries, you pass a kiss.
When your sons worry, you flash a smile.
When your women wave, you ignore them.

A BIOGRAPHY

Poetry cripples. *Tempus fugit.*
Have removed from the lit'ry wars
the hand of a gentleman in quill,
the blackberry ink mixed with tears,
who sought the ingratitude of his day
as a sculptor, clay or an alchemist, brass.

Poet or poem? Life or art?
He cared for his judgments in their prisons,
he likened himself to a convict,
he lifted his vision to the window,
he dug for the treasures of light,
he entered the solitary's tunnel.

Women he loved he surrendered,
as leaf falls for the love of leaf.
Felons he insulted and readers perverted.
In the cave of the senseless, it all fit:
the thin shafts the stars shone down
could not lighten his life at hard labor.

THE PORNOGRAPHIC BUT SERIOUS HISTORY

of myself, begging your pardon, as a
young man, quick to draw arms, quick
to take a fence for daggers toward my
heart, quick to shoot from the hip,
fast to let fly in all directions
as if to injure fatally the unsettled

just recognized in myself, which is why
in the end I take myself for example
though what the new critic says isn't proof
and the thin line is shifting again
between comic and tragic, body and spirit,
and the wife doesn't know her husband.

Not to fill up with history but no ideas,
not to merely *see* life and think it images,
not to think morality a bad medicine
does the husband offer his boyhood to his
wife's mouth, the words are a white balm,
the self heated to the temper of its time.

II

THE ESCAPE INTO YOU

YOU AS DESTINATION

I inventory services: your ass
in position, shudder thrust or circle,
peace you are at before or after
to bring me to, whereas formerly
I lay on my back, a wide-eyed child,
and the ceiling a relentless press.

I thought, as a child, it would kiss me,
would crush me—it was not unlike a spider,
flexing its four spread knees (where walls
met), and I played a happier game too:
spreading by lash or fingers the light
into star-columns, endless energy and sky.

I couldn't know how many light-years
your message might take, or if you had one,
playing my kids' games, kidding the scary
dark which meant adult lives, meant life,
drawing down a ceiling-full of fear:
hairy times, horny times, and still you there.

I ADORE YOU (1960)

What to include?—I borrowed money
from you, rubber bands, like
a rubber band space in your bed, we
banded together. Turned out, forever.
Lust piece, collar and elastic,
I'm glad I was up to participate.

I took time off from work, wife
on the way out, took to you candy
flowers, bittersweet grounds for mid-
morning Mexican divorce stemming
adultery from. Living conditions improved
because receptive to my advances.

In all those pastorals, teetering sheep,
when the wooden lover stubs his
badly extended heart wanting mother.
Not us. Though my father was just dead,
Mother thought you an angel:
down from heaven, up for grabs.

THE RING

A puzzle for keeping, four bands
woven like collegiate lives we led
toward, interlocked when apart.
The new achievement of the pure
white page was the absence of
pseudo-disaster of young first marriage.

But not for vice in the flowers
nestled in your hair, we survived
trust, truth, archaic seats of wisdom;
wasn't it a chair
we felt for, back from business,
your ass more than others found it.

Furniture dictated every move,
our mistress-library
of master editions like a double yoke.
We collapsed on overstuffed affections,
wedding puzzle on my finger, I gave you
the answer: good and plenty.

THE ESCAPE INTO YOU

Eight years of making it, who deserves
that many more, like a reprieve
from war the week-end soldier
furloughs into a medal of dishonor?
It wasn't enough to be a mountain,
you had to be a river I couldn't swim.

We had your body to build on.
Even that arranged a little paranoia
like a face you almost once
recognized over a raincoat when
the elements came together, you
swearing, what a gasp to see an old friend.

A slut could have broken my heart,
the way we lived. The event, for all that,
was so special I never asked, Are you,
or are you not, overcome by my fast
glandular diabolism, huh? Soldiers
leaped; I loved your silent stones.

1968

A MEMORY

The first wife floats in memory calmly
who formerly was storm-tossed, who gave
at the edges a whitewash to those rocks
on which she would founder, who founded
the Territory Hysteria, bordering
the knife, the state of the doomed union,

who spent lavishly the genital coin,
who ate up the year's best and its worst,
who was the slaveship that came in,
who wasted the fortune in the hold we
have mentioned, who put out for history
a veil of tears, and a sour milk steam.

Recall, also, how you arrived by that ship,
seasick and blubbering as much as anyone,
and how it took you, for all its wooden groans,
to land, and then let you leave.
You were the dullest coxswain alive.
You were put in the hole for good reason.

THE AUCTION

We sold the chairs from under your
suffering, then the squeaking sagged-
in-the-center four-poster baby farm,
and the bureaus of inflamed information:
the chest of personal effects containing
left-overs we had no longer stomach for.

No piece deserved packing the past—
the crazy oracular goodness
of my first wife notwithstanding
—after which I hoped you would inquire,
to be answered by poems and totems,
and a blonde boy: by her, for you.

These facts, too, were just furniture
we could sell away, or break and burn
in the long winters of Great Depressions.
Ashes to ashes we faced each other,
out of which bidding this song is reborn
for you—for which, forgive me.

YOU, HEAVENLY

We whipped the priest alright,
and cut off the Rabbi. When young
lint-free missionary Mormons
in black went door-to-door in block,
I showed them to itchy straw seats
under prints of your behind.

Really, these were photographs
of wondrous half-moons, or just
of light as it took pieces of you.
I meant nothing dirty, and didn't
tell them even when they asked
what my camera'd used for model.

After all, I loved religion,
taking for my model the image of
the Lord, which is the example of
you, magnetic head, ass to South.
Some people were embarrassed by this,
who mistook the ass for a mouth.

HOMAGE TO ALFRED STIEGLITZ

The address of the equivalent
is in the cloudy mind though also
"out there." You must face it.
One bush, a thousand faces.
So there is also camera-work in love.
So there is also work.

But the mind wants to dwell on the body.
In New England, in winter, in long ago,
the faces of evil
were seen, severally, by hard-working
settlers though cold suited them.
The truth would set them on fire.

Once, in a field of vision,
we were acting without persistence,
and in a room with one light let
the buffeted optics of beauty
into my camera. The idea was dizzying:
I could never expose you enough.

THE COAST

Even if they'd announced it
("Not just a back for a shirt,
a fork for the trousers, and a long-
handled mask to fuck from,
but he sings it."), even if the muse her
self lay down for my pillow,

still I missed you Westward like sin.
Finally you are the whole contour
of my *safety* on the peaks of risk of
my own making, and in depression
you post my notes to the frivolous:
Out of Town; Out of His Head Upstairs.

Holding back by coming on, if long
out of Egypt but into bondage,
promised nothing, I found ways to you,
I don't want out, ever, of this interior.
You are the ships, as well, I secure to,
and his majesty's defense like a halo.

THE DRIFTING

Who called a crisis a spade?
—which unearths to the root canals
down which one man you took for god
paddled his own canoe. Not you.
You were assaulted from above:
that God, making up for good times.

So I loved you from underneath;
you wouldn't look down
when you floated to shores
of no light you washed up upon,
looking for my shoulder, rib, one
hand, joints rolling caresses.

I was drowning, using the dead
man's float like a call for help
down that stream of gold that wound
round you: half a jacket for me
but a ring for you. Everyman a Houdini
who escapes that water with his wife.

III

THE DAILY GRIND

*Meta*physical, not pornography,
to say we balanced each other.
Some thought it bad to exercise
unless trying to have children.
If we had a thousand, it wouldn't
be enough but just crowded.

On a lonely isle, you are
my idea. In a slow dream of going
across China, you are company.
But still I don't love you
because I have no choice.
I love your voice

saying nothing but moans,
no eyes, no moons: pushing the black
back by the virtues of your sex,
which are those parts of you—
heart but one, and that figurative—
I enter into I love.

THE DAILY GRIND

How to account—if you can't
on your fingers the charge the current
stores in the blankets, say, between
two people who contact their chests,
for what happens next, and didn't you know
what they were fucking for?

The deepest penetration, legs drawn,
as if for bicycling, up, occurs because
he requires at this juncture her total
submission, hard work's worth this much
HE WAS THINKING when he laid off
his secretary at great personal cost.

Every lover's a poor lover. Every piece
of tail's a story of hard times.
Still, you're a sucker for her body.
Like a nail into your conjugal coffin,
you drive it into her, closing fast, thinking:
what was it better you were going to leave her?

IN THE HOME

Nothing in thick clothes is
happening, no grounds for divorce
this time, no one breaking down the
last rung in the ladder of lusts
propped against the house of bonafide fidelity
no one can enter but must prove residence.

If a step on the stair
is a fist in the heart,
if one treads carefully
on the ego and the heart in the hand,
if the song in your heart is my heart
in your mouth—why, that's bloody possible.

What's a metaphor but a mask,
a conceit but a god-awful bore?
Either/or: there's more to be said for slumber
after a good screw: turning in for the night:
with more than a handful of pleasure,
with more than oneself to come to.

RESCUE, RESCUE

I need you like a sailor needs
his hardtack, I have floundered
far from shore away from paradise,
I need you to cut my teeth on.
It's not easy to let you loose,
not to set you up so I'll need you.

I need you when the boat rolls,
when the mast we thought an arrow
snaps; I swim like a stone.
If you're free, I'm over here,
and over here!, and over here!
The better you swim, the more I drown.

I have worried if the lungs can survive
these extra washings, if the heart
won't wrinkle and the hands retract.
What I've given I wouldn't take back.
I wanted something perfect; without me,
the rescues succeed without regrets.

LIGHT POEM

I'm in a phone booth in Saratoga Springs.
The water tastes awful, but very helpful.
You aren't answering, whatever I'm asking.
I'm asking right now why you aren't answering.
It's pleasure, pain, or just love of quiet.
You're not answering; I've got coins for nothing.

I'm going to stamp out my feelings for you,
post them in a letter like a long shaft
brought to your box by fanjet airlines.
On a plain chair, arms flapping, I'm winging
to that heaven of babies, that stellar
interstellar galaxy of persuasions, those

fine passions eclipsed by sunshine
but now, in the dark, all that we see
and all that we ever wished for, swore for,
lied and cheated and stole for.
I'm sending you tomorrow the letter of today,
a little dried-up light from far away.

YOUR SHAKESPEARE

If I am sentenced not to talk to you,
and you are sentenced not to talk to me,
then we wear the clothes of the desert
serving that sentence, we are the leaves
trampled underfoot, not even fit to be
ground in for food, then we are the snow.

If you are not what I take you to be,
and I am not what you take me to be,
then we are the glass the bridegroom smashes,
the lost tribes underfoot, no one sees,
no one can speak to us, in such seas we
drift in we cannot be saved, we are the rain.

If I am unable to help myself,
and you are unable to help yourself,
then anything will happen but nothing follows,
we eat constantly but nothing satisfies.
We live, finally, on the simplest notions:
bits of glass in the head's reticent weather.

THE MAKING WAY

The husband's ribs like the tree
you might have lived under
give you protection everything comes through
whether solace or mercy,
whether relation of blood or word of mouth.
The ear is oppressed to be so cared for.

The crickets sing their rounds endlessly
until someone approaches.
Then, in the silence, there comes to say
There is an end to the random,
a moment which requires your departure.
You press your seal of goodbye against him.

O what will he do with small children,
or with no one to keep his company?
That's not what he affords
by letting you go, but bountiful harvest.
He doesn't fall, but bends a little;
he gives you a way to the light.

THE EMBRACE

This song for you is full of shark,
this indiscretion, like graffiti,
is made public to please you. Fine lady,
can we come together, fish who rise
from prey, who scribble in the temporary
waters the line of greatest resistance?

After the first ear, I fainted.
Nobody wants you when you're down
and out. Clip the tender parts
together, they said. Joined. Holy
because married. Nobody escapes this life
together, who gets away from himself.

I suppose walking into water until too
late, I imagine the clothes neatly bent
in a nearby pile the body floats from.
I imagine the horror with which I find you,
discovering downstream the day before yesterday
how much you loved me to hold on to.

FROM THE WARDROBE

Collecting hearts, drawing you out—
like the billowy message the pulleys
whined between ledges, for which
you stood undressing, for which no one
objected long to showing the tongue so—
I shuck the thick skin just by talking,

sometimes. But sometimes the clothesline
sags with labor and lucklessness—
the faded house prints, the making-do—
and you see in these tenements nothing
of the young girl whose hair was a river
her lover set sail on, and out from.

And if the sails are sooty sheets now,
and if the pulleys creak to go nowhere,
what is that on the ocean?
The woman abandoned is an old story
the gulls will not feed on.
Every so often, you must dress it up.

WE HAVE KNOWN

We have known such joy as a child knows.
My sons, in whom everything rests,
know that there were those who were deeply
in love, and who asked you in,
and who did not claim a tree of thoughts
like family branches would sustain you.

My sons, in whom I am well pleased,
you will learn that a man is not a child,
and there is that which a woman cannot bear,
but as deep wounds for which you may hate
me, who must live in you a long time,
coursing abrasively in the murky passages.

These poems, also, are such and such passages
as I have had to leave you. If very little
can pass through them, know that I did,
and made them, and finally did not need them.
We have known such joys as a child knows,
and will not survive, though you have them.

IV

ON UTILITARIANISM

Vision doesn't mean anything real
for most of them. They dance
beautifully way out on the thin limbs
at the top of the family tree,
which we have admired for
its solid trunk and unseen roots

we know go back to other countries
where "God help us" was a prayer
one planted like a seed, staking everything
on labor, luck and no concessions.
All of us remember the rains that year
which exhausted the Czar and the Bolsheviks.

Hungry, wet, not yet sick of ourselves,
we escaped by parting the waters;
we brought this black bread to live on,
and extra enough for a child.
That bread didn't grow on trees.
We multiplied, but we didn't reproduce.

SONG OF SOCIAL DESPAIR

Ethics without faith, excuse me,
is the butter and not the bread.
You can't nourish them all, the dead
pile up at the hospital doors.
And even they are not so numerous
as the mothers come in maternity.

The Provider knows his faults—
love of architecture and repair—
but will not fall into them for long:
he can't afford the adolescent luxury,
the fellowship of the future
looks greedily toward his family.

The black keys fit black cylinders
in the locks in holes in the night.
He had a skeleton key once,
a rubber arm and complete confidence.
Now, as head of the family, he is
inevitably on the wrong side looking out.

THE ANSWER

I give the black pit dream's head,
not fearing to hit bottom, to the water
I offer my head like a stone,
just as my tongue enters silence
a thick air collects in both ears,
and then I'm in Heaven like a piece of dirt.

What did we think we came to?
A mountain? A molehill? A farm? A well?
Well, we are a little bit of gold after all,
and a small share of lumber and weed.
You could stand outside the owner's gates
for days and yell to cause nothing.

He's hardly ever home. Where he is,
the owl is derisive, and the cow sad.
The bird is too heavy to fly, the fish
too bloated to swim, and men like us,
drowning in words and dreams, thrash wildly
to build up the answer.

WAKING EARLY

Agony of babies in the fog-clot,
creep of sweat, young grasses singing,
morning of indecision we must eat,
kernel of gristle, stomach-knot,
liver congealing to stone, lead for
the feet, we rise, we stumble—no—walk.

Rhishh of wind through paper, then growl
of wine bottle and can and burnt-out shoe
at grate-mouth of gutter: our corner
where we pass from loneliness to nothing,
a bread of carbons, glassfuls of acids,
crop-killers, preservatives of the spoiled.

Poetry here is a halter; the workers, horses.
We will be given our skin for paper,
if we must have it. We are given sick blood
for writing. The ache at the crotch
as our life drains. What did we want to say,
that the mother means, calming the babies?

THE EINSTEIN POEMS

Fall, and the sick elms pour themselves
into themselves: funnels for DDT, passage-
ways for the fallen, alms for the poor.
Where once there were robins, dry rot;
where there were beds, misery's company.
The legacy's writ large in Railroad Gothic:

a funereal invitation a spider's patience
could not have knotted in the lushest garden
except he stitched it through his own bowels.
Fly into that web; it will gut him.
In that deep cave, love's a last meal
you will never wash your mouth of.

You would eat flowers if the flowers were
healthy, you would dine on the sidewalks
if the concrete had some specific purpose,
you would flush your insides if the water
were holy, you would love your neighbor
if he would help you help it help him.

ON UTILITARIANISM

Everyone wants to feed everyone else.
Piled in back alleys, bread greens
antibiotics of its soft centers,
money foments yeast reaching the moon,
change turns into silverfish kids drop
gum for. We cast it on *these* waters.

We turn rubber into trees, flowers,
make a cow of loose leather, a sow's ear
of a ruined purse, we change wine to blood,
bread into flesh, as if there were no tomorrow
we change men into women, alter the course
of the stars, we try to beat the odds.

The odds remain; the chances come and go.
Peace in the backwoods is deep in that nature
we long since baptized and confessed to
we wanted out. Now that we are free of the woods,
we try making that forest for the future
in the city where there's no tomorrow.

GETTING LOST IN NAZI GERMANY

You do not move about, but try
to maintain your position. Would you eat
the fruit of the corpses?—You would.
Your friends are the points of a star
now a golden, unattainable "elsewhere"
because there is no elsewhere for a Jew.

Men have closed their daughters to you,
and now the borders like neat hairlines
limiting your ideas to hatred and escape.
This way, they have already begun
the experiments with your brain—
later to be quartered and posted.

Cremation of what remains?
In a dream like this one, a weathered face
will drive you off under a load of hay
at the very moment the Commandant calls.
You could swear the voice you hear is kind,
calling you home, little Jewboy in alarm.

THE CHILDREN

The death of the father is my shepherd,
he maketh me three versions of wanting.
He giveth back my shadow; he restores.
He pays out and pays out the darkness.
How much does it cost to keep silence?

How much does it cost to keep calm?
It costs my brother his heart like a sleeve.
It costs for the children with no hearts.
It costs in the stomach, when it is kicked in,
on the flaming arms of the infants,
jelly to jelly it costs in the mother's ovaries.

We are the just gypsies dictators hate.
We contain the hate and wrap it in a warm
blanket of babyfat, while the bones
wait in the children's graveyard at the Capitol.
Or here they come walking!, hands joined by chains,
on the cobbled *Calle de Niños Heroes*.

If their rags embarrass you, will you wipe your noses?

V

INTERLUDE:
INSTRUMENTS
OF THE LORD

INSTRUMENTS OF THE LORD

More I sing, or would, I promise you.
Every Jew can be a cantor,
but he is usually hoarse. The ineluctable
modulations of the intellect bam bam bam
are majesty (the transmission of wings)
and begging which makes one sore.

Who was minding the store
during High Holy Days, if not God?
If on Sabbath the treasuries closed,
wasn't that better than bestial sacrifice?
Though his tongue be long, still
the ox can't blow the shofar.

The masses are no asses.
All we desire, Lord, is a good excuse!
Jews were always in this world,
waiting for a son or sign of the next.
Until he provides, God our Father
sends us fortune to be our stepfather.

OUR ROMANCE

The road is narrow which leads to that house
we have lived in and then eaten like candy.
These were the stories we digested,
and no wonder. The roof was sweet,
the chimney was gum, the mortar was butter,
the end was in sight.

We were the children. We came home at night
to a big bed near a bright light,
and someone bigger just down the hall.
The owls were wise, but we were knowing,
the dark wasn't coming up from downstairs
so fast we couldn't sleep through it.

The children's song would cut its throat;
our hearts, soil our sleeves; yet
how could we know? We were tidy and various,
like jars of preserves in a row:
we saved the children, playing parents;
and saved the parents, being children.

LOVESONG

Even cream in a wound would hurt
like salt: an idea about catching
birds' tails becomes love's other idea
that the lady likes pain for herself
if the hurt be enough for one only.
O she is his only one, to be hurt.

Birdsong rested during flight.
Then the cardinal sang tree to tree
to his mate springing into free
air the excitation of the promised.
She would be his; he, hers. Under
leaves we watched, on whom would fall.

A season's time's real landscape
where we live, and snow covers us
who were willing then to do anything
in warmth where we pleased. Then please
listen, Dear. If I should hurt your ear,
it's not the music's fault to be fair.

SEED AND SERUM

O felicitous hazards like sharks
entering the blood, afloat on rubious
swallowing, hopelessly hungering for
nourishment of tragedy pulsing!
"Women's troubles," difficulty of
hemorrhaging, loss of blood you've had.

And endured birth like stolen
luggage, stayed in that country where
trauma attends every meal
like a tiny culture kept warm
by faint touch of heart. Then
took fear to those waters daily.

These losses of health, like asthma,
may be breath of death,
or Edenic visitations by the Father.
Still I invoke the nuptial evening
rites of doctoring; and, past all nights,
in a low bed our deep recovery.

SERVICE FOR TWO

These rose-colored glasses—effacement
or dissolution, for example, of hunger:
the aerated bellies I would fill.
But the worm flowers in the very earth
which grew inside us to be taken back
to the green sheath we lie down in.

The plural of silver is always silver-
ware, static tine after tine poverty
feeds upon, failure of alchemy to fix.
Like cone inside cone, the mouths
widen as they draw nearer, exchange
circles and point their opposite ways.

We only wanted to fill up with pain
on the crumbs of love, not these dumb
animals which enter our blood daily.
Hunger surmounts hunger; the spirit
spits on the body; the heart chews
on the heart, for the sake of the other.

THE MUSIC OF THE SPHERES

Hard knowledge to come by. Finally,
the greatest satisfaction is to survive
not as knowledge or music
but on *this* sphere as old magic.
The black highlights take away parents
and friends in old story, style of mystery.

Who goes there?—among gravestones
could crush you, ground give way under,
and all the time the dead
reacting like fiber in an earth of bed.
Hard to see your way, that doesn't help
to *see* help or know old love buried.

Still, these were something to stand on,
bodies we held to, and hold to,
to whom we were told to
promise small favors, and we didn't.
They gave us guilt and the past,
and we sing what we know best.

(SEA SAW)

The leg doesn't need a rung to stand on;
the heart doesn't ask for pity for itself.
It pities its neighbor, the small intestine,
once considered too ugly for providence,
fit for a devil's measure only, now gone
off the reservation to whoop the meter.

We could go out whaling for ribs, digging
for applause, clamming for open hands.
Old Uncle John will take us aboard,
he doesn't think he's anything special.
The bachelor crabs will reverse their field,
the bass will wash up for tidings.

O it's cold cold cold at the bottom of the sea
and my true love's freezing,
and my true feeling's dying,
and my true nature's showing,
and my words are all drowning,
and my love is very gorgeous (at the bottom of the sea).

WHAT THE DOCTOR ORDERED

Sutures for the forked tongue,
twine twice-round for the heart.
Seals, approval, steamy backing.
It was in your head all along—
the way you spoke, the new skin
of growth and your "broken" heart.

Perhaps you imagined even *her*,
whose fairy kisses are psychogenic:
warts, deep vacuums, low aches.
It's not likely love should last
in this world, which does not pardon us,
by this sun no one may look at long.

From beauty, I have gone blind.
And here give in to all darkness.
The questions I asked of stones
will not be answered, the light
not shine in the eyes of the beloved
except I think I see it, and I do.

THE FIGURE

Your hair, falling, becomes that road
we have travelled but lately come to,
without replacing the body.
The heart is a gummy, bellowing organ,
sucking and sending to the wrist
blood for a cat's-paw—wailing, wailing:

a song to stir us to likenesses. Thus,
your eyes have their wings, your
nails their glamorous moons, wrists
have their ratchets, and tongue its spring.
Your legs offer choices, your deep-seated
love gives me room to maneuver.

Each piece of you is something else
your therapeutic body sings to me;
you hamper travel resourcefully.
Good heart, screw, love for one or two,—
this, and the dough from your flaming oven,
is what a man can live by.

VI

CONSTANT FEELINGS

TIME PIECE

Time is money. *Caveat emptor.*
If death travels "here" to "not far,"
still that failure is a long process.
In the New World, wonder loves you
no better than I do, little Puritan,
that time you were living a life of hard knocks.

The silence had a personal edge
but we climbed the full height of the other
and asked of those shoulders the possible,
those white—yes, white as lilies!—breakers
spoiling our view of the constant
delirium close up to the coastline.

Now the vast correctable purity,
though we wished always to search inside
for the channels of our prolonged agony,
of your naked stretching diverts me.
Your fulsome ass on the pillow is that
New World we sailed over the edge for.

.

THIS DEEP

What can't we say, and why not?
Is it these objects, such studied
couches and carpets wherein we sink,
the raised arm disappearing downwards
with its fisted message of going under,
as if this were water for smooth sailing?

The portside leans, the starboard leaps,
we topple the length of the rope rail;
the bell is hard in the wind, the wind is
soft and inviting and slaps us with a glove.
The glove is death, like the last of a costume
death makes it complete in this air, moving.

Death is moving.—We are self-conscious.
We have made this house our ship, we have
also seen each other as boats to come in.
From the death of the planet, which is a boat,
in this air which is a sea, in language
bubbled from the deep, we swim and say, "swim."

THE BODY POLITIC

There is less to say than ever
now that your sweet ass, spreading
from the luxurious punishing,
and your positively wonderful tits
which have become tipped bullets,
have come into favored positions.

It is true that probably circumstance
permits us no choice about destruction,
and that we must become pieces of plates
and lucky whatnots like rubble we walk on,
but still I'm happy, actually giggling
like the sound of a fountain in Florida.

How many oranges will fit in a carton,
how many grapefruit (large) in a sack?
And does a *non sequitur* necessarily follow?
Me?—I've got the lumps of the sun,
the books of the Big Daddies, intestines
like roads taken, and you North and South.

THE OLDEST CHILD

Nathan proceeds by his head as through
stone walls, or an arrow through a conduit,
but the substance of this pointed love
cuts deep channels a bucket couldn't touch:
is bloodletting and heartbreaking,
and the crush of bone wanting breath.

Nathan proceeds as if he believed everything
will be alright if we can put on the thimbles,
it will be ok when we cover the candles
and so move into the dark without weapons,
alright when the white weave of intentions
is brought to surgery in the poem.

Nathan helpless before his soft insides,
Nathan with "real" and "natural" mothers,
Nathan like water to whom ice has closed off
the avenues of escape, Nathan goes forward
past stars, fathers, dark to his own lights.
His glands swell; his hurt heart hardens.

Fish
are the soul of delight.
You can never be better than your father.
The knuckles the face makes
bring you up short in the water.
Did you come here to drown?

The flowers would eat anyone
if it meant a living. Spring the locks!,
loosen the belts, down from the roof:
the *borshch* is getting colder
and my father is getting older,
late father is getting older.

One wants a song for Mother,
since what we eat we are. Mother,
it's me, calling from under the water
for a hot meal and memory's candle,
for fish, feather, foul and man,
for a stone that would reach me.

VIRTUOSO OF THE X

Bunched up by magic, huddled together
in a far circle the bombers will pass
on their way to more radiant targets, . . .
I would provide that jewelled incantation
recently worn and recently repaired
and lately in danger on which the world turns.

We turn to each other. To cloudy prayer.
We watch out for the signs of a cheap joy.
Everything is dear, which once was free.
What is the cost of a rag for a charter?
How far must we go to gain an inch, what's
asked and measured, who has his ruler?

These are secondhand questions, Love,
not quite fit for human habitation.
Better lives are missing in the pitted gears,
an aroma of gas remains in the showers.
If I pull the tides of the moon by my thumbnail,
will light stream through this costume jewelry?

3 STANZAS ABOUT A TREE

1: The tree, too, wants to bend over
and wait a million years for an agate bridge
itself may have become, as we
turn and turn into, with final grace,
that seamless singleness we could not embody
across the river in our own bodies.

2: The tree has bent over which carried
us here, striations like glyphs from
who-could-imagine, and there were plenty,
too, who came for the sun,
who now are burnt into the earth
in a black seal familiar to but one or two.

3: Have we a vault for fury, a cathedral,
like the redwood? Have we wanted to be glass
or a diamond of the first water? That oak
has the same date with carbon we have.
Have I (think!) wanted to be the tree, or
one, two or three stanzas about a tree?

WHAT LASTS

So help me, Love, you and I.
Paper into pulp, and our words last
as ashes to cool the sun.
The pen lasts in stories by the fire,
the ink bubbles, the word is cremated
and spreads dumbly as in our lungs.

I wanted to speak it now. And how
the explosive sound of the lungs,
collapsing as they give back air—
we have had that energy, burning.
We have been at the throat of the world.
We have had a lifetime.

I concede to that blue flower, the sky,
a more than passing moral guidance.
Because light flashes, dies, flashes,
some sing the rhapsody of the liver.
Yet what the symbol is to the flower
the flower itself is to something or other.

THE DEFEAT OF THE INTELLECT

We have boxed it into a corner, where
it snarls and writhes in a terrible odor
burning rubber could not cover.
It hates us, in its furry outer logic,
as a child hates its father
in guilt, for guilt, when it is time to.

Now it is time to fly at the center,
to become the arrow. We will feather
the eye of the target, enlightenment
like a jar of fireflies for keeping
small worlds lit. They are like white
pills, the chaste ladies of fast fortune;

the light we can divide and conquer.
But there is another light, beyond
the jar, the shining bodies, the world
we can say, it surrounds the love we
do not luggage, like an Egypt full of
Jews it makes no sense.

CONSTANT FEELINGS

Some acts I could never, not
forthrightly, not by flanking
you, accomplish, like that bridge
the poet tried to put in his poem
to be put in his pocket (another
became a bearskin, already shed).

I wanted to harp on that bridge,
of course to be that bluebottle, corn-
flower, the three leaves of the sassafras.
Naturally I hoped the coat of my arms
would, when I reached for you, spin off,
revealing the new skin of a purer animal.

I think I shall always love you.
When I enter your skin, I am closer
to bear, bridge, bush and that tree
which, granting the lovers shade,
will be my veins round yours: many loves
which are lives, but do not depend on lives.

SONG: THE ORGANIC YEARS

Love, if nothing solid rises like wood
above this scratching, this waxen cane
of a tree, if nothing from this trunk
unflowers after long reaching, if finally
the leaf relaxes its bodily processes,
at least we had a hand out to help it.

Also, you have carried me far on your
way into the earth, in the prophetic
imagery of your tunnels I was satisfied,
and in your lovely arms I lay weeping
the truth. If belief doesn't make up
for the long argument of life, still

we made up with what was natural. Now,
from the long, blind alleys of learning,
and in the winter of metaphor, our arms
reach like branches toward the light, our
roots go down to clear water, our fingers,
so long counted on, are not dry yet.

THE WILLING

I am not yet ready to die inside,
while the ash founds a society of its own
rooted in the clean dirt, while
the berry tree signals its neighborliness
and the weeping willow says "forgive."

Mister of the chapel, Mister of the steeple,
who says go there when the road is a ladder?
I have to take that promise myself
which ended for so many without flowering
and sit the branches and the buds through

storm of birth, whipping of circumstance,
lacerations like birthdays in the garden.
Surely foliage needs this beating of foliage
to aspire to: the winds effacing the trees,
the open spaces up ahead pleasing danger.

OBSESSIVE

It could be a clip, it could be a comb;
it could be your mother, coming home.
It could be a rooster; perhaps it's a comb;
it could be your father, coming home.
It could be a paper; it could be a pin.
It could be your childhood, sinking in.

The toys give off the nervousness of age.
It's useless pretending they aren't finished:
faces faded, unable to stand,
buttons lost down the drain during baths.
Those were the days we loved down there,
the soap disappearing as the water spoke,

saying, it could be a wheel, maybe a pipe;
it could be your father, taking his nap.
Legs propped straight, the head tilted back;
the end was near when he could keep track.
It could be the first one; it could be the second;
the father of a friend just sickened and sickened.

PUT BACK THE DARK

Let's not stop in cold, in drought,
but blanket and seed our own bed.
We'll be a long time dead.
We walk now on stilts, on dagger heels,
through the howling of impatience
and the ailing imprisoned.

We walk now through the jails,
nothing to provide, a notion of being
free leading us from these helpless,
away from ambition and vanity,
toward the comfort of solitude
like a tree living two-thirds in death.

There is nothing left to resist,
where there is nothing irresistible.
So these poor cities fade from vision
not maniacally but as an old memory
which was not important to that dream
when your hand into mine put back the dark.

It is not incumbent upon you to complete this task; neither are you free to desist from it.

Sayings of the Fathers
The Talmud

Marvin Bell was born August 3, 1937, in New York City, and grew up in Center Moriches, Long Island. Since the fall of 1965, he has been on the staff of the Writers Workshop at The University of Iowa.